Investing

Investing. It is something that many people only dream of being able to do. They think of it as some sophisticated way of earning money. They even believe that only the smartest and wealthiest of people are able to invest. They find themselves watching the stock market wishing that they could get in on just one great deal.

The good news is that they can. Today, you don't have to be rich in order to invest in the market. You don't have to be a genius in order to get hefty returns from your investment. Investing Basics: Learn the Stock Market, Build Passive Income, Grow Your Wealth is going to show you exactly how you can start investing in the stock market in order to grow your wealth.

In Investing Basics: Learn the Stock Market, Build Passive Income, Grow Your Wealth you are going to learn how you can start investing today with very little money. This book is going to teach you everything that you need to know in order to get started making money in the market.

From learning how to determine what investments are best for you, to diversifying your portfolio, to seeing your first return, this book is jam packed with information. You are going to learn about Penny Stocks, Micro-Investing, Dividends, Yields, Bonds, Stocks, and so much more.

When you have finished reading this book you are going to be ready to start investing your money in order to grow your wealth and build a passive income. This book was written so that you can learn everything that you need to know in order to start investing as soon as today.

You are going to learn exactly what you need to do in an uncertain market, how to reduce your risks when you are investing, how to invest in a way that will provide you with another income and more!

This book is going to teach you investing strategies that you need to know in order to build your wealth. It is going to help you to understand how you can protect your investments even when the market is not stable and how you can choose the best companies for you to invest in.

By the time that you finish this book, you are going to be able to start choosing companies that you want to invest in. You will be able to create your investing plan and you will know what your investing goals are. You are going to be confident as you start investing in the market, knowing that you have put your money into companies that are going to provide you with returns.

You will also know how you can protect yourself from some of the most common mistakes that beginner investors make, how to protect yourself from scams, and how to get started investing as soon as today.

This book really does have it all when it comes to investing. If you want to see a great return, if you want to set yourself up for success, build wealth, and create a passive income, this book is for you!

Investing Basics

Learn the Stock Market, Build Passive Income, Grow Your Wealth

information is without contract or any type of guarantee assurance.

Table of Contents
No table of contents entries found.

Introduction

Investing Basics-Learn the Stock Market, Build Passive Income, Grow Your Wealth contains proven steps and strategies which will help you learn how to invest so that you can grow your wealth and build a passive income while reducing the risks as much as possible.

Throughout this book you are going to learn all about investing in the market. You will learn tips and tricks that will help you to reduce your risks, while increasing your chances of seeing a hefty return.

While many people still believe that investing is only for those that are already rich, I am going to show you in this book that investing is for anyone. You do not have to have a million dollars to start investing. In fact, in this book you are going to find out how you can start investing today with very little money.

You are going to learn how to choose which stocks you are interested in purchasing and how to determine if they are good investments or if you should walk away from them. You will learn how to get the best returns on your investments by ensuring that the stocks you purchase are growing.

This book is going to teach you how you can prepare to invest your money. Did you know that there are certain financial steps that you need to take before you start investing your money into the market? This book is going to show you exactly what those steps are so that you can ensure you are financially ready to invest.

Many people avoid investing in the market because they are afraid of the uncertainty of the market. We watch the market go up and down every day. It seems like something can happen on the other side of the world and affect the market which makes investing seem very risky. However, there are steps that you can take in order to reduce the risks even when the market is uncertain. Which means that while other people may be losing money or may be too afraid to invest, you are still seeing returns.

There is so much information jam packed into this book that it is sure to show you exactly what you need to know about investing in the market, from learning about penny stocks, to hedge funds, to diversifying your portfolio, and more this book has all of the information that you need if you are interested in investing.

Stop putting it off until tomorrow. The best time for you to start investing is right now so let's get started!

Chapter One: What You Need To Know Before You Get Started

The stock market is on the rise and from the looks of things it is only going to keep rising. In fact, as of the time of this writing, the value of the New York Stock Exchange is over 21 trillion dollars. Maybe you want a piece of the action.

If you are like most people you probably think that you do not have enough money to start investing. Maybe you think that you don't know enough about investing to make any money in the market. I have a secret to tell you: it is very easy to make money investing in the stock market. In fact, anyone can do it.

Before we get started learning how to make money in the stock market there are a few things that we have to go over.

The first thing that you need to understand before you can start investing in the stock market is what the stock market really is. The stock market is nothing more than a marketplace. It is a place with buyers and sellers just like Amazon. Instead of them buying and selling a product though, they are buying and selling stocks.

A stock is a piece of a business. When you purchase a stock, you are purchasing a piece of ownership of that specific business. For example, if you were to purchase Walmart stock, you are purchasing a piece of Walmart.

Before the stock market existed, if you wanted to purchase a piece of a business you had to find out who the owner was, track them down, get into contact with them, and then make them an offer. This was a very time consuming as well as complicated process. After all of that work was done you were not guaranteed the opportunity to purchase a piece of the business.

Today we have the stock market where with just the click of a couple of buttons you can purchase pieces of any of the businesses that you want.

The next thing that you need to understand is that there is a difference between investing in stocks and trading stocks. Trading stocks is very different than investing in stocks and it is not a very reliable way for anyone to make a profit.

When a person trades stocks they will usually own the stock for a very short period of time and quickly trade it. Trading stocks means that you rely on predictions and chart patterns to know when to trade.

So often people decide that they want to get into the stock market because they think of it as some glamorous and very easy way for them to make a lot of money in a short period of time. The truth is that for most people trading stocks is a game that they will lose at.

Why? The people who tend to trade stocks have been making their living on the stock market for years. They have a lot of experience and when you first get into the stock market, they have the edge. It is very hard to compete with them. Even though it is possible for a person to make money by trading stocks, it is very unlikely that it is going to happen. So, while trading stocks sounds like a really sophisticated way of making money, I would give it some thought before risking all of my money.

Investing on the other hand is completely different. When you invest in the stock market you will purchase stock and then hold on to it. Sometimes people hold on to the stocks for a very long time. This is done so that when the company reaches its full potential you will be able to sell the stock and get the most profit possible out of it.

Instead of trying to understand technical analysis and compete with long time traders you are simply reading the company's annual reports or financial statements.

When it comes to investing in the stock market it is the small investors who tend to have the edge. Success is seen in stock market investing because an individual investor is able to keep a hold of the stock for a very long time.

A professional fund manager cannot do this because they want to keep their jobs, they have to be able to show on their reports every quarter that they have had returns.

What is great is that as a small investor you have access to all of the information that the big-time traders do. You can learn everything that you want to know about the company that you want to invest in before you ever put a dime into the company.

Coming Up With Investment Ideas

The easiest way for a person to come up with investing ideas is to think about the different services or products that you use in your day to day life. Then you can look at the different businesses that you can invest in.

When you wake up in the morning what is the first thing that you do? Do you have a cup of coffee? Would you like to invest in Folgers?

What is the next thing that you do? Take a shower and brush your teeth maybe? Have you thought about investing in Colgate?

Next you probably get dressed. Perhaps you would like to invest in a clothing line.

As you go throughout your day you will want to continue to take note of each of the products that you use as well as the services. For example, if you stop at Starbucks before heading to work, you may decide that Starbucks is a company that you would like to invest int. Where do you get the gas for your car? What about your lunch? What is your favorite grocery store? All of these are businesses that you can invest in.

It is amazing how many ideas you can come up with by just paying attention to the products and services that you use each day. The great thing about starting with these companies is that chances are you already know a lot about them. You do use their products and services after all.

Starting with the businesses that you know is a great way for you to begin learning how to invest. Choose one business and start learning everything that you can about them. This is so much easier to do when you actually like the company that you are learning about.

This approach is also going to ensure that your investing is going to align with your personal values. If you drive an electric car for example, because you want to reduce your carbon footprint, investing in the company that made your car makes more sense than investing in a company that does not care about the environment.

It is important to know that you cannot purchase stocks in private companies. Every company starts out as a private company but once they reach certain requirements investors and traders are going to be able to purchase shares in the business via the stock market.

The majority of companies that are well known are companies that you can purchase stock in. There are a few, such as

PetSmart, Airbnb, Sephora, IKEA, and others that are still private which means that you cannot invest in them.

Once you have created a list of companies that you would like to invest in you will want to narrow the list down by removing any of the companies that are still private. You can find this out by using Google.

Simply type in "Is (the company name) publicly traded" into the search bar. Google will let you know if you can invest in the company or if it is still private.

How To Tell If The Stock Is A Good Investment

When you buy stock in any business, there is no way for you to know for sure if it will perform well. When most people purchase stock, they do not worry about whether it will rise or fall in the next year because this is not how wealth is built. When you are investing in a business you have to understand that it can take years for your stock to reach the price where you want to sell it.

When purchasing stock, you want to make sure that you are buying it at a price you are willing to pay and that you are willing to sit on them for a while. When investing in any company you want to make sure that you:

1. Know how the company earns money. It is astonishing how many investors are willing to risk their money by purchasing stock in businesses that they do not understand. Before you purchase any stock, you should be able to explain to anyone how the company makes a profit. You should also have some understanding of the major cost inputs. For example, if you are thinking about investing in a company that produces tires, you need to know how the cost of the materials used to make the tires is going to affect their profits.

2. Does the company have a competitive advantage? The majority of people are not going to care what brand of screw the local hardware store carries. However, they are going to care if the store that they shop at carries the brand of toothpaste that they use. They will care if the store provides them with different brands to choose from. If you are thinking about purchasing stock in a store, Walmart, for example, you need to be sure that they have the competitive advantage over other stores. Are their prices too high? Do they provide customers with the brands that they are looking for? Those types of questions matter.

3. The company is going to survive if the economy suffers. The economy goes through ups and downs. It is during the down times that a lot of companies go out of business. You do not want to invest in a company that could go out of businesses if the economy goes south because you will lose all of your investment. It is fine if these businesses grow slower than other businesses. Remember you are in it for the long term.

Are You Ready For The Stock Market?

Finally, before you decide to get into investing in the stock market you have to determine if it is the best option for you given your financial situation. Is there another place that you should be putting your money before you start investing in the stock market?

Sure, investing in the stock market may sound super sexy and like it would be a lot of fun but it is a long-term investment. On average, if you invest wisely, you should expect to make a 7 percent return on your investment. This means that if you invest 100 dollars into the stock market and do it wisely you will have 107 dollars at the end of the year. Not an additional 107 dollars, an additional 7 dollars.

But what if you have credit card debt? If you are paying a 20 percent interest rate on your credit card debt but you are only making a 7 percent profit. This means that you are still losing money.

The best use of your money then would be to pay off your credit card debt before you start investing in the stock market. If you are in debt, you may not be ready to start investing in the stock market. While it is understandable that you want to start investing in the market now, your profit is going to be much larger if you pay off your debt first and then invest.

I know that many people will tell you to get into the market as soon as possible but you have to really give it some thought to determine if you are ready and how much of your money you can afford to put into the market.

Start by thinking about the expenses that may come up over the next year and then five years. There are things that you must do in order to prepare yourself financially for investing. You do not want to invest all of your extra income into the market if you have not set up an emergency fund yet. You do not want to end up putting yourself in a tough situation because you have sunk all of your extra money into the market.

You also need to think about your other financial goals. Do you want to buy a house? Do you want to buy a car? The money that you are saving for these items cannot go into investing in stocks. Remember investing is long term. You do not want to invest your money in stocks if you plan on pulling the money out after a short period of time and purchasing a house you will not make a profit this way.

When you think about long term investing when it comes to stocks, think 30 years or more.

Start an investing account. After you have paid all of your bills, put money in your emergency fun as well as the savings account for whatever large purchases that you plan on making such as a house, then you can budget a certain amount to your investing account. Once you have a little bit of money built up in the investing account you can invest it.

Anticipating expenses is going to ensure that you do not end up pulling your money out of the market at a time when you are going to take a loss. This is going to ensure that the money can stay in the market until you are able to make a profit then if you decide you that you have to pull out you won't risk losing your money.

Terms You Need To Know

Investing is a wonderful way for anyone to build their wealth. However, before you start investing you have to learn the language. That is, if you want to be successful.

Risk- You will read this word a lot throughout this book, but you are going to hear it even more once you start investing. It may seem as if the word itself is pretty straightforward, however, it gets used in a couple of different ways when you are taking about investing.

To make things easy, risk relates to purchasing power loss that could happen. Every investment is going to come with some risk. Some of them that could seem very low risk in the short term, can increase in risk over time. For example, if you keep all of your money in the bank, not in a savings account, just in the bank, it comes with a very low risk short term. On the other hand, when you think about inflation, just letting your money sit in the bank means that your money is actually losing value. That's a pretty big risk.

When you look at risk this way, you are looking at how much of a chance your money has of losing value from the time you obtain it to the time that you are ready to spend it.

As you can see, everything that you do with your money involves risk. Some risks are just bigger than others. Stocks for example, have the potential of providing you a much better purchasing power, however, there is also the chance that your purchasing power could decrease.

Return- When an investor uses the word return, they are talking about the money that they get back from the money they risked. For example, if a person were to invest 1000 dollars and they got back 1,100 dollars, they have a return of 100 dollars. A return can be positive, or it can be negative. In order for a return to be positive a person must make money on their investment. If the return is negative, they have lost money.

In order to determine whether the return that you get is good you have to think about how long the money was invested. On average a person can get back between 9 and 10 percent each year in returns in the market. This means that if you got a return of 10 percent in 9 months, it was a very good return. However, if you got a 10 percent return after 5 years it is not a good return at all.

Option- Options have no value on their own, however, hey get their value from something else. An option is a contract that ensures an investor can purchase or sell 100 shares of their stock (the particular one is named in the option) at a specific price before, or on the date that the option expires. A call option allows the investor to buy. A put option allows the investor to sell.

Options are generally used by more advanced investors because it is possible for you to end up risking more than you have invested. This means that you have to be very careful when thinking about using an option.

Capital Gain- Whenever you sell one of your investments for more money than you invested, the profit is your capital gain. On the other hand, if you sell one of your investments for less than what you invested in it, your loss is called a capital loss.

Capital gains are not something that is guaranteed when you are investing. The chances of you receiving a capital gain is going to depend on the success of whatever company you have invested in but also on other conditions that affect the market such as war or a recession.

Cost Basis- This is the amount that you paid for your shares. For example, if you have purchased 100 shares at 30 dollars per share and you paid 30 dollars in commission, your cost basis would be 3,030 dollars.

When you decide to sell your shares, you have to include the commission and any other fees (your cost basis) when determining your gain.

Mutual Fund- This is usually the first type of investment that people will make. Most often, that is because mutual funds are what are offered by their employers or because their broker recommended, they start there.

Mutual funds can help a person to diversify their portfolio very easily. We will talk a little more about diversifying your portfolio a little later in this book. The disadvantage of a mutual fund is that they tend to be very expensive and you have to take care of the taxes even if you are just holding on to the shares.

Index Fund- This is a type of mutual fund that mirrors the market. Index funds tend to buy and sell their shares less often than regular mutual funds do. They are also much lower in cost. Because it is so hard for mutual fund managers to beat the market average, index funds may be a better option for you.

While there are many other words that you will hear on a regular basis while you are investing, these are the most common. Knowing these words will help you understand more about what your broker is talking about. It is also going to help to reduce your risk when you are investing which is extremely important. You want to reduce your risks as much as possible.

Chapter Two: Getting Ready To Invest

As you think about and prepare to invest in the stock market which hit record highs, there are a lot of things that you have to take into consideration. Investing in the market is not something that you want to do on a whim. You want to make sure that you are prepared and that it is something that you are going to be able to do.

Investing in the stock market is a great way for you to take small investments and create wealth for the future. You may want to start investing so that you can begin creating a cushion that you will use when you retire.

It is in your best interest for you to not depend on your investments to put your children through college or pay for your entire retirement, remember there are always risks when investing, but you can use your investments to create wealth to make your future better.

Using these 8 tips, you will be able to start making smart investments in the market no matter how much money you earn.

The first thing that you are going to want to do once you have decided that you want to invest in the market is to set your budget. You do not want to jump into the market without first taking the time to understand how much you can realistically afford to invest.

When you are first starting out, you do not want to try to invest more than 5 percent of your extra income. This means 5 percent of whatever you have left after all of your bills are paid. If you don't know what that number is, it might be time for you to create a budget in order to find out.

The next thing that you want to do is exactly what you are doing right now. You want to make sure that you take the time to learn as much as you can about investing. At the very least you are going to need to know the basics about investing.

You will want to understand what the potential growth of each type of investment is. For example, stocks, bonds, mutual funds, and CDs. You need to know what to expect when you invest in them.

Don't stop at just learning the basics though. You want to make sure that you are setting time aside every day to focus on learning as much about investing as you can. The more that you know about investing, the more likely it will be for you to succeed.

Creating your goals is the next step. You need to start thinking about what you plan on getting out of your portfolio. Your portfolio is created up of the investments that you hold. Your shares, mutual funds, hedge fund, bonds, CDs and so on. Think about your goals. Do you want to invest aggressively in order to be able to get a huge return for your retirement? Do you want to make small investments that will grow over time? Knowing how you want to invest is going to help you to create your goals.

If you want to make money by investing you will have to learn how to focus on market trends. This is going to help you learn where you want to put your money. The great advantage that we have today is that technology helps us track these trends which makes investing much easier.

You do not want to put a lot of pressure on yourself when you are first starting out. Instead, you want to make sure that you are setting yourself up for success. Think about your goals over the next year, five years, and even ten years.

It is important for you to know how much of a risk you are going to be able to handle. If you were to lose 1000 dollars would it take a huge chunk out of your investment fund? If this is the case, you need to be very careful when you are investing.

Because your tolerance for risk is so low, you are going to have to make sure that you do a lot of research to ensure that you are not putting your money into a company that is high risk.

The good news is that if you are long term investing, the majority of stocks do go up over 10 to 20 years. When you are investing you may find that you have to deal with the emotional rollercoaster that the market can cause. This is why it is so important for you to make sure that you are honest about how much you can lose.

If you are the type of person that goes to the casino and gives up after losing 20 dollars, you are going to want to focus on easy investments instead of more aggressive ones.

Once you know how much you can lose and what your goals are, you will want to focus on finding your investing style. Some people want to transition into making all of their income off of the market. If this is the case, you will want to focus on watching the market and taking the steps slowly in order to become a full-time investor.

Other people are going to have the ability to allow their investment time to grow. For example, if investing is a hobby or something that you have started to do simply out of interest, you may decide that smaller investments are for you.

Make sure that you understand all of the fees that come along with investing. Most of the time when you move your money from one place to another there are going to be costs. There are brokers who can help you when it comes to buying and trading smaller investments.

You have to make sure that if you get involved with a mutual fund that you understand management fees. This cost covers the pay for the people who ensure that the mutual fund grows.

Sometimes the fees that go along with different types of investments dictate where a person is willing to invest. Some of the fees can end up costing you more than you had anticipated which is why many people are wary of mutual funds.

You need to find a broker. Your broker needs to have your best interest in mind, and they need to be within your budget. You don't have to worry about using a broker that is extremely well known if they are out of your budget. Instead, focus on finding a broker that few people know about but is an expert in the field that you are interested in investing in.

The broker should be confidant in their abilities, and they should listen to what you want. If you feel like you are not being heard by your broker or that they do not have your best interest in mind, start looking for someone else. The broker needs to know what you are able to risk, what investments you prefer as well as the types of industries you would like to invest in.

If your broker starts investing your money in companies that you have no interest getting involved with, you may end up becoming very frustrated, even if you get some returns.

When you are investing, it is very important for you to make sure that you are keeping your emotions under control. Keeping control of your emotions can be a hard thing to do when you are investing, especially when you are just starting out. You do not want to get too excited about your returns and end up investing without putting in the proper amount of research.

This happens all of the time. A person will invest, see a good return and then end up investing that return in something they would have never invested in before. When they end up losing their money, they become upset, feeling as if they are doing something wrong.

Never do anything based off of how you feel. Your emotions are just that, emotions. They are not going to help you make good decisions. If you do get a good return, give yourself enough time to really consider what you want to do with that money.

Continually making smart decisions is going to allow you to see more returns which will allow you to invest more and will improve your financial outlook.

While there are a lot of people out there who have had a lot of luck in the market, you have to remember that none of them have a perfect record. Everyone who is investing is taking the same risk as you are and everyone who is investing is hoping for a profit but that doesn't always happen.

However, when you follow these steps that we have just talked about you will increase your chances of success in the market.

Chapter Three: Uncertain Market

Today more than ever we have to understand that events that happen across the globe can affect every part of the globe. It can cause our market to be uncertain when there are threats of war, a financial crisis, recession, or other economic events. It seems as if every country is affected by the smallest crisis that another country faces. This can make our market uncertain.

Of course, any time that you are investing in the market you are taking a risk. When you purchase stock, no matter how much research you have done there is going to be some level of uncertainty.

When there are threats of war or a global financial crisis, companies are unable to predict their earnings accurately. When this happens, investors take their money out of these businesses and invest them in businesses that they consider much safer. Because of this the stock market can depreciate.

When it comes to an uncertain stock market, the uncertainty is caused from the inability to predict what will happen in the future. There is no way for a person to predict how severe a recession is going to be or how long it is going to last. There is no way for anyone to predict what companies are going to be affected the most in a recession and what companies will go under.

Most companies, even in times of recession will continue to predict their sales and their profits as if they were in normal market conditions which means that these predictions cannot be relied upon. They are inaccurate.

Uncertainty in the market has an effect on the economy as well. For example, if there is a threat of a recession it is likely that people are not going to be running out purchasing nonessential items. Instead, they are going to be holding on to their money, trying to save as much of it as possible in order to ensure that their families are able to make it through a recession.

When there is uncertainty in the market companies start laying off employees in an attempt to combat a decrease in sales. As a result of a threat of a recession, and the fact that people are no longer purchasing nonessential items, companies that produce these items tend to lose investors.

The economy is also affected on a much larger level. For example, if there is a threat of war, we often see the world's oil prices increase dramatically. This results in gas prices going up which then affects businesses that have to transport their goods. This leads to the stocks being affected as well because the businesses are not able to make as much of a profit as they would if gas prices were lower.

Strategies For Investing In Uncertain Times

When times of uncertainty in the market arise the best thing that you can do is to stay as informed as is possible. Make sure that you are keeping up with how the market is being impacted as well as researching how specific companies are growing.

Learn which companies have the most to gain and which have the most to lose in the event that a recession takes place. An uncertain marketplace has creating amazing opportunities for investors to take advantage of if they are in the right position to do so.

Some investors are going to decide to start looking for companies that will continue through the recession and will purchase stocks at a very low price. When the economy turns around, they make huge profits.

It is very hard for a person to risk their money in the market when there is economic uncertainty. It is very possible that you could lose the money that you invest, however, it is also possible for you to reap huge rewards once the market turns around.

Many people choose to move their money in to safer investments during an uncertain economy and that is fine to do. If you do have enough money to invest in companies that you are sure will make it through the uncertain time do it because your return is going to be very high!

Top Strategies You Can Use

1. When you are investing whether it is when the market is doing great or when times are uncertain you do not want to make your decisions based on your emotions. Many times, when the market is uncertain people make decisions out of fear. Any decision made out of fear is not going to be a rational one. If you are afraid right now, step away for a couple of weeks and let the market do what the market does. Then come back and think about investing. If at some point you find that you have already started investing and fear is guiding your decisions, take a step back and leave the market alone. You don't have to pull out right now. You don't have to make changes at this very moment. Don't sell your stocks because the market has dropped you are only going to lose money if you do this. Stick with it. Remember you are in it for the long haul.

2. When the stock market is uncertain spend your money investing in more tangible assets. For example, when the market is uncertain you can purchase houses for very low prices. Real estate is a great investment and it will help you to not only protect your investment but make a profit along the way.

What do you do? Grab up a few houses when the prices are low. Fix them up but don't go overboard with a bunch of fancy amenities. Find some renters. You will want to be very careful when it comes to renting out your properties. I have seen so many property owners rent properties to people who destroyed them. You do not want to let this happen. You can do inspections on a regular basis to ensure that this does not occur. Make sure that the wording in the lease ensures that if any damage is done to the property the renter will be charged for the repairs and so on. Once you find a suitable tenant, you will be able to rent out the property. Usually for more than what you are paying for it.

What has happened is that you have taken money out of the market in a time when the probability of losing it was very high and have invested it into something that is tangible.

Later when the economy is strong again you can sell the houses, or you can continue to rent them out making a profit from them. If you sell the houses, you can turn around and put that money right back into the market.

3. Stay safe One of the biggest mistakes that people make is investing everything into the stock market. Do not invest your retirement or your entire life's savings into the stock market. Even if the economy is booming you could end up losing everything.

4. Invest in other things besides that stock market. Don't put all of your eggs in one basket in other words. Instead of putting all of your money in the stock market, open up savings accounts, get a fixed annuity, or purchase bonds. This is going to ensure that you are not going to end up losing everything that you have invested.

5. Don't sell your stock when the prices bottom out. It is natural to want to get out of something before you lose everything that you invest, however, you do not get involved in investing in the stock market to lose money. There are going to be times when you watch your stocks go from being worth a lot to almost nothing. Don't pull out. Stick with it and you are going to see that the market is going to go up again.

If you are going to sell, make sure that you do so when the market is high so that you can make the most out of your investment. You can put the profit into another account, or you can reinvest it in the market. Or just let it sit there for 30 years and see how amazing your investment can do.

When you follow these tips, you are not going to have to spend your time worrying that if the market tanks you will lose everything that you have worked for. You don't have to worry about going broke because of the market. Using these tips is going to ensure that you are prepared to stick with investing long term and get the most profit out of your investment.

Chapter Four: Knowing the Company You Are Investing In

When thinking about stock, a lot of people think about it in the same way that they think about gambling. It feels to them as if they are tossing some money in a pot and hoping that they become rich overnight. That just isn't how investing works though.

Purchasing a stock does not meant that you become the owner of a shiny new piece of paper, but it means that you are now part owner of the company that you purchased stock in.

For example, if you purchase stock in Apple, you are now a part owner of the Apple Company. If the company earns a profit over the next couple of years you are going to see your share price go up which means your profit is growing.

On the other hand, if Apple did poorly over the next couple of years then your shares value would go down meaning that you were losing money.

As simple as this is, many investors are not taking the time to learn important information about companies before they invest in them. This means that they end up investing in companies that cause them to lose money over and over again.

You want to be part owner of a company that is going to be successful, one that is going to give you a good return on your investment. So of course, it seems only natural that you would want to put in the necessary time to learn as much about the company as you could.

Don't worry this is not as complicated as you are thinking that it is. Learning just 8 bits of information about any company can mean the difference between earning a profit and losing your entire investment.

1. The CEO- The CEO is much like the captain of the ship. He will steer the company in whatever direction it is going to go. He will decide exactly what people underneath him are going to do which is going to determine how successful the company is going to be.

The first thing that you need to know is who the CEO is. When you find out who the CEO is you are going to be able to learn more about them and the businesses that they have run in the past. This is going to help you determine if you want to invest in the business that they are running right now.

Once you find out who the CEO is you will want to ask yourself if you feel that they have the experience that they need in order to run the business that you are considering investing in for the next 10 years. What have they done in the last 10 years? Did the CEO of the car company that you want to invest in run a retail chain that went out of business? Why did it go out of business? Is there a chance that this CEO could cause this company to go out of business? Do you feel comfortable with the person that is running the business? What about after the CEO leaves the business? Is it still going to be able to do well?

2 The business model is the next thing that you are going to want to look at. There is no perfect business model, but it needs to be a model that you understand and one that you agree with. For example, we know that Wal-Mart offers the lowest possible price to their customers in order to sell as many products as possible. While a company like Coach does not make as many sales, because the sell fewer products at a much higher price, their profits per product sold are much higher. What about Dollar Tree? They sell all of their products for 1 dollar. How well do you think this business model would

work in a time of recession versus when there is an economic boom? Would it still be worth purchasing stock in Dollar Tree if there was an economic boom?

3. I mentioned the competitive advantage a little earlier in this book as something that you wanted to think about when you were purchasing stock. Let's look into it a little more. A competitive advantage simply means that a company has an advantage over its competitors because of either: brand power, patents, superior products, operating efficiency, or advanced technology, or a mix of any of these.

When you are considering investing in any company you want to make sure that the company has the competitive advantage. We know that Walmart's competitive advantage is that they offer products at prices that are very hard for their competitors to beat. What about Coca-Cola? They have the competitive advantage over smaller brands of Cola because they are a very well-known company and they sell a variety of products that consumers love. They are a company that is hard to compete with. When a company has the competitive advantage, they are going to be a more profitable company and that means that in the long run, they are a better investment.

4. Revenue or the amount of money that any company makes from its sales is that next thing that you want to learn about. This can also be called the top line because it is the amount of money that is listed on every income statement at the very top.

You want to make sure that the revenue for the company that you are considering purchasing stock in goes up each year and has done so for at least the past couple of years. Not ever company is going to see their sales increase every year you want to make sure that you are not investing in a company that is struggling or whose sales are treading downward. If you notice that the sales of a company have gone down over the past few years this is not a good place for you to invest your money. Chances are that their sales are going to continue to follow that pattern until you lose all of your money.

5. You also want to take a look at the bottom line, or the net income of the company. This is how much the company made after all of their expenses and their taxes were paid. Of course, you can find this on the bottom line of their income statement. You want to find a company where the bottom line is increasing each year. This is going to show that the company is growing and that the company knows how to sell their product while controlling costs.

6. The profit margin is what percentage of the company's revenue that is a profit, after all of their expenses, taxes, and interest has been paid. In order to find the company's profit margin, you will take their net income and divide it by their total revenue.

You want to invest in a company that has a profit margin that is staying steady or increasing each year even in years of recession. This is going to show you that this company is able to sell their product at a higher price than other companies are because consumers are willing to pay that price for the product. Take Apple for example, they are able to sell their devices for a much higher price than their competitors are. This is because consumers are willing to pay that price for their products.

Wal-Mart is another example. Their profit margin has stayed steady because they are able to keep their prices low which brings customers back time after time. Even when there are recessions Wal-Mart is able to keep their profit margin steady.

7. The company's debt is something that you need to take into consideration when you are thinking about investing in them.

Almost all companies are going to have some sort of debt however, you want to make sure that they have a low amount of debt compared to their equity. You want to make sure that you are investing in a company that is going to be able to repay its debt. The lower the debt to equity ratio is, the less of a risk it is for you to invest in the company.

8. You want to find out if the stock is overpriced before you purchase it. Stock is just like a car; you can pay too much for it resulting in you being underwater no matter how good the company is doing. This is called the price to earnings ratio. You will want to find a company that has a price to earnings ratio that is the same or lower with the overall market price to earnings ratio which can be anywhere from 14 to 17 normally. A company that is run well and has a low price to earnings ratio should be seen as a good investment. You may even come across some great bargains this way.

While following these rules is not going to guarantee you success every time it is going to help reduce your chances of losing money in the market. You want to make sure that you find companies that you not only understand but agree with from a business and leadership perspective. You want to make sure that the business has strong management and that they are financially healthy. You also want to ensure that you are getting the best value for your money. This is how you become a successful investor.

Chapter Five: Can Investing Provide an Income? Strategies You Can Use.

Some people want to invest in the stock market so that they can create a steady income. In other words, not all investors are going to want to take the risk of making a huge profit or hitting it rich in the market.

It is possible for a person to create a steady income by investing in the market. In order to do this, you will want to focus on purchasing stock that is going to pay dividends. Dividends are usually paid each quarter to the stockholders.

When it comes to purchasing stock, you want to make sure that you are not confusing dividends with interest. Today most people are very familiar with interest. We know that this is what we get paid when our money is put into a savings account over a long period of time. Interest is also something that we have to pay to those that loan us money.

Dividends are what is paid to the owners of the company, the shareholders. Dividends are the payment that an investor will receive from a company that they are invested in. The dividend is paid from the profit that the company generates.

This means that if the company that you are investing in does not make a profit you will not receive a payment. Dividends can be paid in different ways. Some companies will pay out quarterly while others will pay twice a year. The majority of this time it is paid in cash.

In order to receive pay out you have to own the stock before what is called the ex-dividend date. The dividend date is usually one day before the record date that the company has sat. This means that the dividend dates can be different for different companies.

If you purchase stock on the dividend date or after that date you will not receive any payment on the next dividend payment date. In order to get the dividend, you have to purchase the stock before the ex-dividend date.

You can find out what these dates are on the company's investor section that is located on their website.

Example:

If you own 200 shares of a company and each of them cost you 10 dollars (you have invested 2,000 dollars), and you purchased them before the ex-dividend date, then the company issues a dividend of 10 cents you will get a payment of 20 dollars.

When you purchase the stock before the ex-dividend date you are going to be entitled to your dividends no matter how long you have had the stock from days to months to years.

You may be wondering if it is all worth it but there are actually traders out there who only purchase stock before the ex-dividend dates in order to get the dividend payments instead of focusing on capital gains.

You are going to want to also understand what a dividend yield is. This refers to the most recent dividend payout for a year.

For example, if the price of a share is 10 dollars and the company is offering a 30-cent dividend, (3 percent) an investor that owns 1,000 shares is going to get a 300-dollar payout.

If you are trying to earn an income through the dividend payout you will want to pay attention to the dividend yield for the companies that you are thinking about investing in.

Why Is Yield Important?

When you are investing your income in order to receive a payout from the dividend you have to consider the amount of money that you are going to be making and then compare it to other alternative investments.

The yield is going to allow you to look at the income that you expect to make from that investment. You are going to, by looking at the yield be able to understand if the stock that is 50 dollars and has a 2.50 annual yield is a better or a worse investment than a company that's stock is 100 dollars with a 4.00 dividend.

If you look at the dollar amounts for the dividends you might think that the second company was a better investment but what if I told you that the first company had a yield of 5 percent while the second company had a yield of 4 percent? You might change your mind about which company you wanted to invest in. Understanding yield is going to help you determine what companies you want to invest in if you are focusing on dividend payouts.

What About Stock Growth?

A lot of the time when people think about dividends, they think of something that is guaranteed. We already learned that this is not really the case. You are not going to get a dividend payout if the company does not make a profit.

What is the best way for you to get the most money back in the quickest way possible when it comes to dividends though? This is going to come down to your investment strategy.

First you have to understand that there is something called dividend growth. This is the rate at which a specific company's dividend grows over a period of time. You can predict how the dividends are going to grow in the future by looking at the past growth. And you have to understand what the dividend yield is, or the pay out that an investor would receive at the current price.

Of course, since this is the stock market that we are talking about there is going to be a lot of different opinions as to which strategy is going to work the best.

Let's take a moment and focus on dividend growth. In order for the dividend to continually grow, the company must be growing as well. This means that the management team is very disciplined when it comes to how they use their capital. Some suggest that companies that continually grow their dividends will usually be high quality companies that have very low debt ratios. It is these companies that many believe are more likely to hold steady through an uncertain market.

If a person is using dividend profits as a source of income it is probably best that they focus on dividend growth because this is going to better able them to keep up with the cost of living increases that we see.

On the other hand, if you need an income for a short period of time and are not going to have to worry about a cost of living increase for whatever reason, the dividend yield may work better for you.

If the dividend yield is fixed, an investor is not going to be able to increase their purchase power. They are not going to receive higher rates. These investments are not going to attract a lot of investors and I would suggest that you avoid them, especially if you are just starting out.

When you think about dividend yield versus growth you can think about it like this: A dividend yield is going to allow you to know exactly how much your payout is going to be. For example, if you own stock in a company that is giving a 3 percent dividend yield you know that you are going to get at least 3 percent. You can count on this happening.

On the other hand, if you are using dividend growth, you don't really know how much you are going to be getting. For example, if you own stock in a company that had 100 percent growth this year but only paid out a half of a percent dividend the previous year, you are only going to be able to get a 1 percent dividend this year. Then what is going to happen? Do you think that the company will continue to grow 100 percent in the following year or the year after that? Maybe or maybe not. This makes it very hard for a person to predict what their earnings will be.

Of course, the best option would be to take advantage of both. Besides adding to your portfolio which we will talk about later in this book, you are going to be able to take advantage of both types of investing. However, what is most important is that you invest in a way that works best for you. Focus on getting the most profit for your investment in whatever way that you see fit to do it.

Chapter Six: How To Minimize Your Losses and Maximize Gains.

No matter what you do and no matter how hard you try, there is no way for you to guarantee that you are not going to lose money in the stock market. The fact is that at some point you are going to lose money. It happens to everyone that invests. Maybe it has already happened to you and that is why you started reading this book. Some people suffer from losses in the stock market without even realizing it because it takes on different forms.

Of course, the simplest form of losing in the stock market, as well as the most painful one is when you are watching the prices drop. When investors see the prices dropping, they want to get out fast but remember what we learned earlier about making emotionally driven decisions. You do not want to make an investing decision based on fear.

Most of the time if you ride it out you are going to see those numbers go up again. Don't sell just because the numbers are dropping because that is how you lose money. That is the number one tip that I have for you when it comes to minimizing your losses.

But there are other types of losses when it comes to the stock market. One of them is lost opportunities. We face lost opportunities every day in our lives but facing them in the stock market can be extremely painful.

Example:

You have purchased 10,000 dollars' worth of stock in a little-known company. After a year of watching the stocks go up and down in price the stock is very close to the price that you paid for it. You may try to tell yourself, at least you didn't lose anything, but you did. You left 10,000 dollars tied up in the market for a year and got nothing back for the investment. If you had taken that 10,000 dollars and purchased a CD at the bank you would have earned at least some money back even if it was a very small amount.

When you are purchasing stock, you have to consider the risk. Ask yourself this: "How much could I earn if I put this money to work elsewhere?" Are you going to earn at least that much money in the market? If you are not than you are losing money by investing that money into that specific business.

When a stock does not go anywhere, you are losing money because you could have invested the money in something else that would have ended up earning you money. While many people do not realize this, it is a loss.

Another type of loss that people face when they are investing is called a missed profit loss. This is when you watch the stock price jump dramatically but instead of selling it and making a profit you hold on to it only to see it decline just as quickly.

There are very few people who are able to determine when a stock is at the top or when it is at the bottom. Because you have lost the chance to sell the stock for a huge profit you can consider this as a loss. You have to think of it in terms of the money that you could have made if you had sold the stock when it was at the top instead of holding on to it.

A lot of investors will hang on to a stock and hope that it is going to recover but it may never get as high as it was again. Even if that does happen, for some reason, investors still decide to hang on to the stock in hopes that they are going to make a bigger profit only to see the prices drop once again.

The best way to avoid this is to not be greedy. Allow yourself to be happy with a good profit and don't try to get every penny that you can out of a stock. If you hold on to the stock when the prices are high instead of selling it, you could end up taking a huge hit just because you wanted a few extra dollars.

No one wants to suffer a loss of any kind when it comes to their finances but especially when they are investing in the market. Make sure that you are not allowing your ego to get in the way when you are trying to decide what you should do with your stocks.

Once you have suffered a loss the best thing for many people to do is simply accept that the loss has happened and then move on. However, there are things that you need to do before you move on to the next deal.

1. Review your decision. You want to allow some time to pass before you look back on the decisions that you made which led you to losing money in the market. Be honest when you look back at the decisions that you made. Of course, you have to accept that you made a mistake and that you lost money but the best way to ensure that it does not happen again is for you to learn from your mistakes.

Think about the things that you could have done differently. Were you motivated by greed? Were you trying to squeeze every penny possible out of the market only to end up losing money? Were your decisions based on fear or other emotions? Were you not focused completely on what you were doing when you made the mistake? Is it possible that if you had acted differently you would have lost less money or maybe not lost any money at all? Take the time to learn from the experience in order to ensure that you do not make the same mistakes again.

2. Sometimes when we take a loss in the market, we have to tighten our financial belts. Losing money is not something that is trivial. You are going to have to do what it takes for you to recoup if the loss was small enough for you to do so. Try to regain the money and then when you are ready to try investing again, remember what happened last time. Don't let the lessons that you learned from your mistakes be lost simply because you are jumping back into the market. Make sure that you do not make those mistakes again.

3. Make sure when you are thinking about the loss that you keep it in context. There is no reason for you to take the loss personally. Remember that you are not the only person that took the hit. Lots of investors took the hit just like you did, some of them may have even lost more money. Just because you suffer a loss in the market it does not make you a bad investor and it does not mean that you should give up. If everyone that suffered a loss in the market gave up, no one would be investing or trading.

The truth is that no matter what we do in our lives, we fail at times. We have two options when we face failure. The first option is that we allow it to tear us down. You can pull out of the market and never invest again. Or we learn from it and become better. You can choose to allow it to make you a better investor.

Going Against The Grain

Investing is something that you do not want to follow the crowd in. One of the biggest reasons that people lose money in the market is because they are focused on what everyone else is doing. You have to focus on what is going to work best for you when you are investing.

Investing is like any other part of life. If you are trying to keep up with Tom, while Tom is focused on doing everything that is going to improve his life, you are not going to be improving your own life. The reason is because Tom's life is completely different from your own. The same goes for the market. You may see investors doing different things in the market and want to join them because they seem to know what they are doing but you know nothing about their financial situations or their goals. Stay focused on your own goals and you will see a profit.

Having a hedging strategy is very important. What is a hedging strategy? A hedging strategy is a financial plan that is going to allow you to avoid losing everything that you have invested into the market. The goal of your hedging strategy is to limit your risks when you are investing.

The best time for you to create a hedging strategy is before the market takes a turn. It will allow you to know, as well as to do what you have to do in order to preserve your gains if something happens, such as a recession that negatively affects the market. You will want to have a few hedging strategies that are going to ensure you are not going to lose everything. Each strategy will be based on the duration of time that the market is expected to fall.

Hedging is something that all investors should know about. It is a way to protect your investment. However, the way that hedging is talked about makes it seem as if it is too complicated for the average investor to do.

The good news is that even beginners can learn how hedging works and what techniques other investors use to protect themselves.

Hedging is like insurance. When a person decides to create a hedging strategy, they are protecting themselves against negative impacts on their finances. Of course, this does not mean that you are going to be protected from every single negative event that could affect your finances however, if you have properly hedged the impact is not going to be as big as it would be otherwise.

The practice of hedging occurs in many different areas of our lives. For example, if you purchase automobile insurance you are protecting yourself against something happening to your automobile. You know that if someone crashes into you, if your car is stolen, or if something else happens to your car, you are covered. You are going to be able to get a new car and your losses will be minimized. Of course, you also know that you are going to have some losses, but they are not going to be as dramatic as they could be if you did not have insurance.

The same is true if you purchase homeowner's insurance. The insurance is going to protect you if your home catches on fire, floods, if there is a tornado, if someone breaks in or if some other disaster strikes. While you may lose a little, it is not going to be as dramatic as it would be if you did not have any homeowner's insurance. Hedging works the same way.

It would be wonderful if we could pay a fee each year in order to ensure that we would not take a huge loss on the market, however, hedging is not that simple. Hedging means that you are using financial instruments or strategies to reduce your risk of being negatively affected by any movement in the market.

Hedging is going to cost you some money. However, you have to remember that the point of hedging is not to earn you a profit but instead it is to protect you from a loss. You have to ask yourself if the cost of the hedging is worth it.

The good news for the buy and hold investors is that you will not have to worry too much about hedging. Because you are planning on keeping the stock for a long period of time you will see the investment grow as the market improves.

Why learn about it? Even if you are a buy and hold investor you need to know how hedging works because it will help you to analyze your investments.

The bottom line is that there is no guarantee when it comes to the market but by using hedging you can minimize your losses. This is going to help you to ensure that if the market does take a nosedive you are not going to lose everything that you have invested in it.

Cash Reserves

Do you remember at the beginning of this book when I talked to you about making sure that you did not invest all of your money into the market? The reason is because of the risks. If you want to reduce your risks in the market, you have to make sure that you keep cash reserves.

Cash reserves are going to allow you to not only take advantage of opportunities when they arise, but they are also going to ensure that your decisions concerning your investing are not based on fear.

Never invest more money in the market than you can afford to lose. Do not invest your entire retirement fund in the market. Do not invest your child's entire college fund in the market. These should be separate from the money that you are investing in the market. You have to make sure that you have enough money put into your emergency fund to get you through hard times, ensuring that you are not prematurely pulling money out of the market.

An example:

Let's say that you have been investing in the market for a few years. Everything that you have is tied up in the market. From the way that it looks things are going great and you are going to be able to retire comfortably because of the money that you are making in the market.

You go to work in the morning, and you are called into your boss's office only to be told they are downsizing, and you no longer have a job.

You now have no money saved. Everything that you earned was stuck in the market. What do you do? You sell your stocks, taking a loss on some of them in order to get by until you are able to find another job and then you have to start all over again.

What was the point in investing in the market in the first place if you had to pull the money out and potentially take a loss?

Let's look at this another way.

You have been focusing on your finances over the past couple of years. You have an emergency fund sat up that has a value of three months of your income sitting in it. You also have a nice retirement fund set up and a separate savings account. You have purchased some stock but have not built up a huge portfolio yet. It is a work in progress.

You go into work in the morning and the boss calls you into his office only to tell you that the company is downsizing, and you are out of a job.

What happens now? You are able to fall back on your emergency fund and your savings account. You are not risking losing your retirement fund and you do not have to pull out of the stock market. You are able to let your stocks sit and grow as you look for a new job. Your family does not have to take a loss because you were not prepared for the unforeseen event of you losing your job.

Another example:

Imagine that you are investing in the market and you do not keep any cash reserves. One day someone comes to you with this amazing opportunity to invest in an up and coming company, the next Amazon for example. You don't have any money to invest because everything is in the market. You have just missed a huge opportunity.

What if you had the opportunity to invest in Amazon when they were just getting started but because you did not have any cash reserves, you were unable to do so. I bet you would be kicking yourself pretty hard right about now.

Of course, everyone that invests in the market wants to make sure that they minimize their losses. Everyone wants to have a good return on their investments and by using the information that you have learned in this chapter you can do just that. You can minimize your risks when you are investing therefore, increasing your chances of getting a good return.

Chapter Seven: Penny Stocks?

Have you ever heard of penny stocks? They have been given a bad name; however, they provide you with the opportunity to make a lot of money. There are of course some cases when the bad reputation of penny stocks is deserved however, I want to show you how you can avoid the pitfalls of penny stocks so that you can invest in companies that will reward you significantly for your investment.

Penny stocks are shares that are usually sold for less than 5 dollars. These stocks are not listed on any of the national stock exchange lists. They can be extremely profitable and are very easy for investors to acquire. However, investors have to be very careful that they do not get involved in penny stock scams.

Pros Of Penny Stocks

Because penny stocks are priced so low, they are very appealing for those that do not have or do not want to invest a huge amount of money into the stock market. If one share sells for just 3 dollars you could purchase 100 shares for only 300 dollars. Imagine how much it would cost for you to purchase 100 shares of a larger company like Amazon. I can tell you that it would cost a lot more money. Of course, penny stocks are much easier for a person to acquire. Penny stocks are recommended for those that are just starting out in investing.

One thing that a lot of investors love about penny stocks is that if they do lose money, what they lose is not a huge amount. If you take the example above, even if the market dips, the only thing that you have invested is 300 dollars.

One of the key advantages is that many people have invested in penny stocks only to see their money grow dramatically in weeks or even in a few days. People have watched the price of the stock go through the roof in a short period of time which has allowed them to get a huge return on their investment.

If you are a first-time investor, the price of many of the larger stocks may be a little overwhelming for you. It can take a lot of money to invest in more well-known companies. If you are someone who wants to start investing, who is learning about the market, and is starting out with a small amount of money to invest, penny stocks may be perfect for you.

When you invest in penny stocks, you will be investing in smaller companies. Of course, getting in on stocks when a company is just starting out comes with its advantages. As the company grows your stocks are going to be worth more and more. Investing in penny stocks is a great way to maximize the return on your investment. You never know which of the penny stocks of today will turn into the next Microsoft, Apple, or Amazon!

Cons Of Penny Stocks

Of course, there are some cons to purchasing penny stocks. Nothing in the market is guaranteed and that includes penny stocks.

When you purchase penny stocks you are purchasing stocks in a small company which means that there is no price stability that comes with purchasing shares in much larger companies. Some companies have been found to make false statements in order to boost the prices of their penny stocks. This is why it is so important that you investigate the company before investing in them. The more that you know about the company the less likely you are to get scammed.

Because these companies are not listed on any of the major stock exchanges there have been a lot of fraudulent practices when penny stocks are being traded. You have to remember that these stocks are not governed by a regulatory body which means that they do not have to make specific information public, like companies in the major stock exchanges have to. There are also no guidelines that they have to follow when reporting their finances. This means that you are taking the risk of losing your entire investment if you do not take the time to learn about the company. It can be very hard for a person to tell a fraudulent penny stock from a genuine one. We'll talk more about this in a minute.

Lack of information is another con. When you think about purchasing a share in a traditional company you know that you have all of the information about the company at your fingertips. However, when you are thinking about purchasing penny stocks, you may not know if the information about the company is real or if it is fake. Most people would start doing research into the company in order to determine if the information was true or not, however, since the company is so new there may not be enough information out there to determine if the information you have about the stock is real or not.

There are also pump and dump schemes out there. The way that this works is that a person will purchase a huge number of penny stocks. Then in order to make their money back or to make a profit they will send out false information inflating the stock prices trying to sell them to investors. People who are using pump and dump schemes will usually contact an investor via a chat room, a newsletter, through their email, or through a press release. Once the manipulator has sold all of their stock to investors, they have made a ton of money and soon the investors find that they have lost their entire investment.

As an investor you have to know when to sell your penny stocks. However, you have to also be aware that it is really difficult for a person to sell penny stocks. It can be hard for you to find a buyer.

If you are planning on purchasing penny stocks and holding on to them for a long time, they could be a good investment. Imagine how much one you would have right now if you had invested in Netflix when the stocks were penny stocks.

These are just some of the pros and cons that come with investing in penny stocks. Penny stocks may not be very popular when it comes to mainstream investors but if you are able to avoid the schemes and get your hands-on penny stocks for a potentially great company, you may end up getting a huge return on your investment.

Spotting A Pump And Dump

If you are going to invest in penny stocks it is important for you to be able to recognize a pump and dump in case one comes your way. You do not want to end up investing your hard-earned money into something that is going to end up causing you to lose.

1. There is a promise of a return. This goes for pretty much everything in life. When someone guarantees that if you invest a certain amount of money you will profit a different amount, they are manipulating you. All over the internet these schemes play out every day.

When someone promises you or even hints at a promise of a high return with very little risk, the red flags should start going up. This is a warning sign that what you are getting involved in is fraud.

You also have to understand that this can be a broker that is trying to get you to purchase the penny stock. Many times, this is why a person would think that the penny stock would provide them with a return. These brokers or firms are not registered. A firm that is not registered is not legally allowed to provide anyone with investment advice nor are they allowed to sell stocks.

2. An increase in trading. Most penny stocks do not get traded often. So if you are looking at a penny stock and notice that there was no trading in the months prior, but suddenly thousands of shares are being traded, especially if it is happening for several days in a row, it is likely that this is a pump and dump.

When you see a big spike in the volume or the price just before you suddenly get this tip about the stock, you should be aware that this is a pump and dump. This is especially noticeable when the chart has been flat for months at a time.

3. You get a random email about a specific penny stock. Often times, an investor will get emails that are promoting different penny stocks. It is never a good idea for you to follow the advice of these emails. This is one of the most common methods used by many different scam artists, including those that are running a pump and dump scheme.

You may also find that you are getting the same tip from a lot of different sources at the same time. This is because these scammers will hire a promoter in order to sell the penny stock and make their profit.

Of course, this is not an all-inclusive list of red flags that you need to watch for when it comes to pump and dump schemes. However, it is important for you to be aware of what can happen if you invest with the wrong person or in the wrong stock.

Penny stocks because of their low prices can be purchased online in large quantities. While it may sound appealing to an investor to purchase a large number of stocks, you have to remember that it is easy to manipulate penny stocks.

Let's think about this for a moment. When it comes to giant stocks such as Microsoft, it would take billions and billions of dollars for these stocks to be manipulated. On the other hand, just a couple of hundred dollars can manipulate penny stocks.

Penny stocks traded on OTC Bulletin Board markets online. While many people believe that it is best to avoid investing in penny stocks, you need to do what you think is best for you financially. If that includes investing in penny stocks, there are some things that you need to do in order to protect yourself.

1. Read the warnings. The SEC has released many warnings about penny stocks for those that are considering investing in them. If you go to the SEC's main website, you can use the tools located there to search for the company that you are considering investing in and determine if there have been any problems in the past.

2. Understand the level of disclosure. Most of the OTC Markets will rate companies in order to allow investors to see how much information the company has provided. The companies that provide the most information are the ones that you will want to consider investing in. Make sure that you do your own research about these companies and don't just go with the information that they have provided.

3. Always look for a financial statement for any company that you are thinking about investing in, especially if you are considering investing in penny stocks. If you find that there is financial information available, you need to make sure that you analyze it very carefully. Research the company online. Find out if any articles have been written by the company and read the stories of others that have invested in the company.

4. There are thousands of stocks listed on the New York Stock Exchange and the NASDQ. If you are not comfortable investing in penny stock, chances are that you can find a different stock on the NASDAQ or NYSE that you can invest in instead.

Becoming An Excellent Investor In Penny Stocks Without Spending a Dime

Before I go into how you can become an excellent penny stock investor without spending a dime, I want to let you know that this technique will work for any type of stock. I suggest that everyone that is considering investing use this technique before they even spend a single penny.

You can use this technique to practice trading all types of stocks including penny stocks in real time without investing any of your money. This is going to help you learn about the market by using imaginary money.

For this example, we are going to focus on penny stocks. The great thing about this technique is that as you learn about penny stocks you are not going to be risking any of your money.

When you are comfortable and understand trading, you will be able to invest your real money. This is going to reduce your risk of losing your investment.

In order to get started you will begin with 1000 imaginary dollars. You are going to want to decide which penny stocks you would like to invest these dollars in. You should think about it as if you are investing your own real money.

In a notebook you will write down what stocks you want to invest your 1000 imaginary dollars in. Write down the price that you pay for them and then you want to also write down when you decide to sell them, including the price per share.

Invest in a couple of different stocks in order to help you get the most experience. Keep track of which stocks profit and which of the investments would have ended in a loss. See if you can figure out what makes some of them profit and why others end up being a loss. When you invest in one that ends up resulting in a loss, you will want to try to figure out what went wrong with your investment.

Continue to practice investing this way, using imaginary money and tracking your investments until you are comfortable with investing. Then you can start making purchases.

You can use this technique for any type of investment. When it comes to investing, practicing with imaginary money is the best way for you to learn. This will help reduce any losses that you would face in the market and help you gain an understanding of how the market works.

Are Penny Stocks A Waste?

How often I have heard people having conversations about penny stocks. I hear one person who does not understand penny stocks talking to another person who thinks they understand penny stocks.

I hear the question, "Why are they penny stocks," being asked and then the answer, "Because the company has no value and does not produce anything of value."

That simply is not what penny stocks are. Many well-known and massive businesses were traded as penny stocks at some point. Some of the shares in these companies are still considered penny stocks because they cost less than 5 dollars a share. Chances are you know some of these companies.

Ford was one of the companies that was once considered a penny stock. They sold for just under 2 dollars per share. Right now, they are still selling for under 10 dollars!

Pier 1 Imports is another company that started out with its shares being sold as penny stock. In fact, each share cost only 10 cents in March of 2009. Investors who believed in this company purchased those shares and in four years they saw the shares go up to 25 dollars. Today each share goes for about 6.50.

Sirius XM shares sold for as low as 3.14 each and today they are selling for 7.16. While they have more than doubled in value, they are still relatively low in cost.

These are just a few examples of the stocks that were once considered penny stocks. As you can see, these are not shares in companies that are unknown or do not produce a quality product. In fact, these are very well-known companies. These are companies that many people would consider investing in long term in order to watch their profits grow.

There are plenty of wonderful penny stocks out there today that you can purchase. As long as you follow the guidelines that you learned in this chapter and do the research that is needed, penny stocks could be a good investment for you.

Chapter Eight: How To Identify A Great Stock

By now you are probably wondering how you are going to find good stocks to invest in. Hopefully by this point in the book you know that the stocks that are going to be good for you to invest in are going to be stocks that are going to increase in value over time.

The bad news is that unless you have a crystal ball telling you what stocks are going to increase over the next six months or year, there is no way for you to know exactly what stocks are going to increase.

It is important to know that most investors do not do well in the market because they are not focused on purchasing the right stock. They focus on purchasing stock that grabs their attention. They may purchase stock that has been in the media or that is followed closely by many investors.

Instead, they need to be focused on undervalued stock. When you are busy investing in the same stock that all of the other investors are investing in, your gains are going to be average at the most.

Of course, no one can blame investors for investing this way. It can be overwhelming to try and find an undervalued stock when you consider that you may have to analyze thousands of companies.

The good news is that you don't have to analyze thousands of different companies.

The first thing that you are going to want to do is to come up with ideas. You are going to want to have some ideas that will lead you to stocks that you can start to analyze. You can use online stock screeners in order to remove all of the garbage leaving you with only the best companies to invest in. Doing this is going to allow you to make a more independent decision as to where your money will be invested. Remember how I spoke earlier in this book about focusing on your financial goals and not the financial goals of those around you?

This is going to allow you to do just that. You are not going to be influenced by what others are investing in and you are not going to allow their emotions to influence you either.

You want to be on the lookout for undervalued stock. A stock, no matter how cheap it is, will not benefit you at all if the company is in financial ruin. In order to determine if this is a company you want to invest in, you have to determine if it is a great company.

This means that they should have greater than 15 percent return on their equity. This is going to indicate that the company is very profitable and that they have the competitive advantage.

You want to make sure that their debt to equity ratio is less than .5 percent. This is going to show you that the company is not taking on a bunch of loans just to stay afloat. If you are focusing on receiving a dividend income you will want to ensure that the company has a dividend yield of greater than 1 percent as well.

Once you have determined what your criteria is going to be (if you don't like what I have provided) you will use an online stock screener. These are free to use, and your goal is to end up with about 30 different companies that you can invest in.

Once you have the 30 different companies that you could invest in, you are going to want to filter out the garbage. You want to determine if in your list of ideas there is a company that is going to be a true gem, one that will outperform the others.

In order to determine this, you will want to look at their profitability. Is their profitability consistent and high? Their net margins should be increasing which means that the company has the ability to increase its prices or it is learning how to produce the product more efficiently.

Their debt levels need to be low. When a company has a high amount of debt they are a major risk. When a company carries a high amount of debt, they can find themselves in trouble if their sales slow down for even a short period of time. You do not want to invest in a company like that.

Now it is time for you to determine which of if any of the companies that you have identified are undervalued. By this point you will probably only have a few companies left to examine.

It is at this point that you want to determine if the price is right. You want to purchase stock at a price that is going to minimize your risk. This means that even if you find that the company does not do as well as expected in the future, you won't be taking very big risk.

The goal is to purchase stocks at a very low price when a company is undervalued in order to increase your chances of generating a huge return. If you want to make a lot of money by investing in the market you have to focus on that low purchase price. You do not want to be purchasing shares for a large amount of money, risking it if the company goes out of business.

Using all of the information mentioned in this chapter is going to help ensure that you are purchasing stock that is going to help provide you with financial freedom. These investments while they do still carry some risk are low risk. If you do end up losing you are not going to lose much and if you end up winning, you're going to win so much!

It is very rare that you are going to find a company that fits all of these criteria, but it does happen, and these are the golden stocks that you should always be on the lookout for. These are the stocks that end up making investors rich beyond their belief.

You can find a few of these types of investments each year if you are willing to put in the work and look for them. If you are finding them often, chances are that you need to be a little stricter when it comes to your filtering criteria.

If you come across stock that looks great, but you are just not comfortable with the price at the moment, put them on your watch list. Keep an eye on them so that when you are able to buy the shares at the price you want to pay; you can load up on them.

Of course, before you make a purchase make sure that you double check your numbers and then check them again. Always make sure that you are certain that you have not made any mistakes and that you are comfortable with the price that you are going to be paying for the stock.

And never forget that you never want to invest more than you can lose into the market. While this is a really good technique for investors to use in order to help them identify stock that they could make a profit from, nothing in the market is guaranteed. Do not spend money in the market that you cannot afford to lose no matter how well you think the stock is going to do.

Remember, war could break out at any time. The oil prices could skyrocket. We could drop into another recession or worse, a depression! Nothing is guaranteed. That leads me right into the next chapter. In the following chapter we are going to talk about the most common mistakes that beginners make when they start investing.

By knowing the most common mistakes that beginners make, you will be able to avoid them, thus saving yourself and your wallet some serious pain.

Chapter Nine: Common Mistakes Beginning Investors Make

When it comes to investing, as in the rest of life, there is no certainty. The market provides us with the opportunity to create wealth by investing but it also comes with risk.

Of course, as with anything that we do in life we risk making mistakes when we are investing in the market. The key to avoiding many of these mistakes is to be aware of them before you start investing. By being aware of the mistakes that are commonly made by beginning investors you can ensure that you do not make these mistakes, therefore saving yourself a lot of money.

1. Panicking When The Market Starts To Drop

This is a huge mistake that many beginners make when they start investing in the market. When investors see the market start to drop, they tend to pull out as quickly as they can. This is the worst time for them to do so. Pulling out when stocks are at the bottom is going to do nothing except cost investors' money. Investors that are in it for the long haul though will come out on top. They do not panic when they see a dip in the market because they know that it will go up again. The best strategy that a person can have when they are first starting to invest in the market is to buy their shares and hold on to them.

2. Letting your emotions take control when you see a big return on your investment is something that many new investors do. They see a big return and suddenly want to throw that money into the market because they feel they can't lose. They are just like someone who is gambling at a casino. They see a big win and then go all in. We all know what usually happens when someone does this. They end up losing

everything. We have to remember that there is only one thing certain about the market, it will go up or it will go down.

If you do see a big return on your investment, wonderful but do not allow your emotions to dictate what your actions will be. Make sure that you take the time to do all of the research that we talked about throughout this book to ensure that you are choosing stock which will provide you with a bigger return.

3. Focusing on Trading Too Much!

If you are busy trading because you are constantly watching the market, focusing on the minute to minute fluctuations, you are not really investing. Trading this way is going to reduce your returns dramatically. Sure, some people will make money but when we think about it in the long term, they are doing no better than they would in a casino.

Real investing means that you are putting money into the market on a regular basis, when the market is rising and when it is falling. It means that you are doing the research that you need to do, diversifying your portfolio, investing in bonds, and allowing your assets to grow over years. How long do you want to hold on to your stock? According to Warren Buffett, the best length of time to hold on to a stock is forever! Keep them for as long as you can in order to get the best returns.

4. Putting All Their Eggs In One Basket

No one has ever found the perfect investment because it does not exist. No matter what company you are investing in, there will always be a risk. This is why it is important to diversify your portfolio. We are going to learn all about diversifying your portfolio later on in this book but for right now you want to make sure that you do not put 100 percent of your money into stocks. Instead, making sure that you have a variety of investments is best.

5. Assuming That Your Home Is An Investment

So many people think of their home as an investment but let's really take a look at this. Let's say that you purchased your home for 200 thousand dollars 10 years ago and you sold it for 250 thousand dollars.

Many people would say that they made 50 thousand dollars but is that really the case? No. It is very likely that you took out a loan on the house which means that you paid interest over the past 10 years, you had to pay for property tax, repairs, renovations, and homeowners' insurance. Chances are that all of that has eaten away that 50 thousand dollars that you thought you profited from the sale.

Don't get me wrong, owning your own home is a great financial decision, however, it should not be looked at as an investment. It is the place that you live, not a substitute for a savings or retirement account.

6. Borrowing Money Against Their Stocks

When you are watching your stocks go up in the market you may find that you are tempted to borrow more money against the value of the stocks that you already own in order to purchase even more stocks.

Some brokerage houses will allow investors that have only a few thousand dollars invested to borrow this way. This type of lending is called margin. However, the risk is very high. If the stocks that you have invested in fall, you could end up being forced to sell them in order to pay the loan off, even if you are taking a loss. Your ability to focus on the long term is taken away. Remember that when you borrow against your stocks you could be forced to sell a great investment at a bad time.

7. Investing With Money You Have Borrowed

So often a person can start learning about the market and become very excited. They will want to start investing right away, but they don't have any money. This will lead them to going out and borrowing money so that they can start investing. They are so desperate to get into the market and sure that they can profit from it that they assure those that they are borrowing from that they will be able to pay the money back in no time. What they don't think about is what happens if they take a loss, which they will end up doing. They are then stuck having to pay all of that money back, sometimes with interest.

Instead, you need to make sure that the only money that you are investing is your money. It should be money that you are sure that you can spare and that is not going to get you into any financial troubles if you lose it.

Far too often new investors try to speculate about what the market is going to do. They end up borrowing money from friends, family, or even brokers and then they end up losing everything.

8. Investing Without Setting Goals

Before you start investing, you need to know what your goals are. Investors who start out working toward a specific goal are much more successful than those who just get into investing for the fun of it or because they want to try and make a little money. Knowing what your goals are when you start investing is going to improve your chances of getting high returns.

9. Investing Without Any Strategy

Besides needing a goal all beginning investors need a strategy that is going to help them to reach their goals. This is going to be the system that you are going to use when you are investing. Your strategy needs to fit your style of investing. If you are a person who does not want to take much risk, your strategy will be to invest conservatively.

10. Not Keeping Winners

One of the biggest mistakes that investors make is that they sell their stock when it has earned them a little profit. Most of the time this means that they end up selling too early because they are afraid that they are going to lose that little profit. This is often a mistake because the investor is not able to make much money. If you think that the stock is going to rise further, wait. The worst that is going to happen is that the stock is going to fall, you will hang on to it, and then it will rise again at some point in the future.

Another huge mistake that many new investors make is that they do not take the time to evaluate their investments. They don't look over the transactions that they made in the past which means that they are missing out on learning a lot.

Take the time to learn about your wins and your losses. Learn how to understand both of them and why they happened. This is going to help you learn how to predict what will happen in the market in the future.

Chapter Ten: Diversifying Your Portfolio

Diversification basically means that you are not putting all of your eggs in one basket. This is the best way for you to protect your portfolio. When you diversify your portfolio, you are spreading your investments out over different asset classes.

This means that if one of your investments or an investment class takes a loss your entire portfolio will not be destroyed. In other words, you won't lose all of your money. This is going to ensure that if you do take a loss you are still going to have capital which will allow you to keep investing and may even help you to recover the money that you did lose.

In order to diversify your portfolio, you are going to want to invest in a variety of different asset classes.

1. Stocks- As we have learned throughout this book stocks are in an asset class by themselves. There are smaller asset classes within the market, which can include foreign stock, small caps, and large caps. Investing in different classes within the market can help you to diversify your portfolio within the market but you can also invest in different industries in order to diversify your portfolio as well.

2. Bonds- Bonds are a good way for you to invest your money and they are a great way for you to diversify your portfolio. Bonds come with much less risk than stocks do, however, the payout is often lower. It is recommended that as you near retirement age, the majority of your portfolio should consist of bonds. This is because the risk is so much less than if you were invested in stocks.

You can make money with bonds even if it is not as much as you would make in the stock market. One of the ways that people make money with bonds is through interest. A bond is nothing more than a loan. You are loaning the company your money and in return they are going to pay you interest. The rate of interest is usually noted on the coupon. Some bonds have what is known as a floating interest rate. This means that the interest rate can go up and down. These are very popular with investors when the interest rate is expected to go up, however, they are riskier than other bonds because if the interest rate falls, so will the coupon rate.

Bonds that have fixed interest rates come with less risk because the investor knows what they are getting into when they purchase the bond.

One thing that investors have to remember when they are investing in bonds is that bonds are not created equally. You have to remember that some of the organizations that are trying to borrow money through bonds may not be trustworthy.

Junk bonds are the riskiest of all bonds. The credibility as well as the stability of the company are going to affect the interest rate. For example, if you purchase a US government bond, the interest rate is going to be pretty low because most investors trust the treasury to pay the full value of the bond.

On the other hand, when a company that is less trustworthy issues a bond, they have to offer a much higher interest rate. In much the same way that credit works. When one person has a high credit score, they have to pay a lower interest rate than someone that has a low credit score. The problem is that when you purchase junk bonds, you are risking never getting paid.

Bonds are going to stop earning interest after they mature. The money is transferred to pay off the bond to the owner. You as the holder will then have to contact the bond agent and follow their instructions to return the bond to them and receive your payment.

When you redeem the bond at maturity you are going to receive the face value of the bond as well as any interest that accrued since the last payment was made. Some bonds do not pay interest periodically and if that is the case when you redeem your bond you will receive all of the interest.

Let's say that you have a bond with a face value of 500 dollars and the interest rate was 8 percent. The bond matured three months after you received your last interest payment. You are going to receive 500 dollars as well as 10 dollars for the interest that accrued over the last three months.

3. Mutual Funds And Exchange-Traded Funds- Mutual funds are one of the easiest ways to invest in the market. They are relatively stress free as well. More investors have invested in mutual funds over the past few years than they have at any other time in history. However, before you start investing in mutual funds, you have to know what they are as well as how they work.

A mutual fund is basically money that is pooled together from different investors. There is a fund manager who is in charge of investing the money that has been contributed. The goal of the fund manager will depend on the type of fund that you want to invest in. For example, if you are investing conservatively, the manager is going to focus on investing the money into the highest yield companies that have the lowest risk.

The benefit of investing in a mutual fund is that they are managed by money managers. The money managers manage mutual funds as their primary occupation which means that they are going to be able to devote a lot more time to finding the right investments for the investors than you would be able to. You are not going to have to worry about analyzing financial statements or dealing with financial ratios.

ETFs or Exchange Traded Funds usually cost less than the more traditional mutual funds. ETFs are going to allow the investor to spread their money around. ETFs are traded just like stock, during the hours that the stock exchange is open. They are another great way for you to diversify your portfolio.

Diversifying your portfolio is going to help you to protect your assets in the event that the market crashes. At first, diversifying your portfolio can sound extremely complicated however, it isn't.

The majority of people are going to put their money into a bank account instead of investing it because they know that investing comes with risk. The thought of investing the money that they worked so hard for is something that fills them with dread. However, once they understand diversification it can help take away some of that dread.

Most people have heard of diversification or diversifying a portfolio. This is the process of investing your money in a way that reduces your risks. Diversified portfolios are going to yield higher returns while reducing the risk of the investor losing all of their money.

You want to make sure that your portfolio includes different types of assets. The assets that we discussed earlier in this chapter are a great place to start. You also want to make sure that you have cash on hand. This is part of your portfolio. As is your savings account and your retirement fund.

You also want to think about choosing investments that have a varying risk. This will help to offset any losses that you see. Remember that while you do want to minimize your risks, you don't want to restrict yourself to stocks that grow slowly. Choosing investments that have different rates of return is a great way for you to increase your return and grow your portfolio.

Make sure that you have short-term as well as long-term investments as well as investments that pay dividends. Bonds will provide you with interest payments and stocks can provide you with a great return on your investment.

Diversifying your portfolio is going to help to reduce the amount of uncertainty that you have to deal with when it comes to investing. There is always going to be some uncertainty when it comes to investing. However, if you put all of your money into buying stock and the market crashes, you have lost everything. If you put all of your money into real estate and the housing market crashes again, you have lost everything. However, when you invest in different asset classes you may end up losing some of your money, but you will still be left with money.

Let's take a look at an example. If it was 2008 and you had invested 55% of your money into US stocks, 30% of your money into US bonds, 10% of your money into stocks from developed foreign countries, and 5% into other stocks, when the market crashed you would have only lost 27% of the money that you invested.

Some people may tell you that diversification is not necessary that it is nothing more than "protection against ignorance" as Warren Buffet said. However, as a new investor, diversification is very important. It will help mitigate the risks that you are taking as you learn about the market. I still have a very diversified portfolio myself and plan on keeping it that way because I do not intend on losing all of my investments.

Do It Again

Once you have focused on diversifying your portfolio you are going to want to make sure that you keep your investments on track by periodically checking up on it. You may find that you have to rebalance. The truth is that you are probably going to need to rebalance at least twice per year. The reason is that if you do not rebalance you may end up with a portfolio that is not consistent with your strategy or your goals.

If you don't rebalance you are going to be missing out on returns which as we talked about earlier in this book means that you are losing. You may feel that your portfolio is doing great and you don't want to rebalance however, you have to remember that just because something performed well in the past it does not guarantee that it will perform well in the future. You also have to remember that the way that your portfolio is sat up is going to affect your returns.

For example, a portfolio that is made up of more stocks than anything else is going to see more ups and downs than one that is made up of more bonds.

You want to reset your mix of assets in order to bring the risk level back down to what you are comfortable with. You may even find that you have to add in more risk in order to get back on target with your mix.

Remember, investing is not just a one and done process. It is something that is going to require your attention on a regular basis.

In order to diversify your portfolio properly you are going to want to create a plan tailored to you. If you have not already done this, you need to make sure that you define your goals and then know what your time frame is going to be. How long do you want to hold on to these stocks? Then you need to look at how much you are able to invest as well as how much risk you are able to tolerate.

Then it is time for you to start investing. Of course, you want to invest long-term, short-term, in bonds, stocks, and in dividends if possible. You want to diversify your portfolio as much as possible. You want to have some investments low risk and some investments that are a bit riskier.

If you have the time to ride out any lows that you may see in the market you may want to consider making the majority of your portfolio up of stocks. On the other hand, if you are going to need access to the money in just a couple of years or you do not have nerves of steel to allow you to ride out the lows of the market, you may want to invest in bonds or other short-term investments. When you do this, you are going to trade the potential of high returns for lower risks.

Once you have selected the investments it is time to start managing your investments. You can do this on your own or with your financial advisor. However, you do it, make sure that you are doing it on a regular basis. Check your investments in order to determine if there have been any changes in their performance and their risk. Do they still line up with your goals?

Revisit the investment switching things up in order to reach the risk level that you are most comfortable with while still getting returns. Many people choose to rebalance when any of their assets move away from their target by more than 10%.

No less than once per year you are going to want to do a refresh. This is very important to do when your financial goals change, or when your finances change. You need to take a look at your investments and make sure that they still make sense given your financial state. You may find that you are able to invest a bit more aggressively or you might find that you need to be a bit more conservative with your investments.

The bottom line is that you cannot diversify your portfolio and expect that it is going to work for you forever. Our lives change every day, businesses change every day, and the market changes every day. This should make it very easy to understand why your portfolio is going to need to be rebalanced from time to time.

You do want to make sure that you are not rebalancing too often because that could end up costing you all of your return. Once a year to two times each year is a good goal to set. Some people rebalance quarterly if they find that their finances have changed enough to do so.

Otherwise, twice per year should be just fine.

Diversifying your portfolio is very important but making sure that your portfolio is working for you is even more important. Always keep an eye on your investments to make sure that you are getting the most return on your investments as you can.

Chapter Eleven: Investment Apps

Micro-investing refers to the newest investing trend that has taken the internet by storm. When a person uses micro-investing, they deposit small amounts of money into their account. These companies vary in many different ways including how they invest and the different products that they offer the user.

The platforms allow their users to deposit small amounts of money, most of the time 5 dollars or even less to be invested. The money can be invested in many different ways and can provide the investor with a return.

Some of the platforms are going to require an initial deposit. The deposit is very small if it is required. Other platforms are going to want you to link your debit card in order to allow you to take part in round up. This means that whenever you make a purchase, the change up to the next dollar will be rounded up and put into your account.

For example, if you purchase a cup of coffee for 1.25, the total will be rounded up to 2 dollars and 75 cents will be placed in your investment account.

Micro-investing is a very easy way for anyone to start investing. You can choose the companies that you want to invest in, or you can let the platform choose what your money will be invested in. The process is very simple, and it can help a new investor to learn the ins and outs of investing. Micro-investing is going to help a new investor learn about their personal finance issues as well. It can help investors learn how important it is to have a savings account while also helping you to learn how to set money aside each week for investing.

Using these platforms is also a great way for a new investor to test the waters. You will not be putting up a large sum of money which means that if you do lose money it is not going to be very much, but it is also going to allow you to see a return on your investments.

The great thing about these platforms is that you do not have to know a lot about investing. You do not have to be a pro at investing in order to make a return. You are also able to invest in different companies without having to purchase a single share. Instead, the money is put in a pool, much like a mutual fund and you will own a portion of a share.

Most of the platforms are going to charge a fee, however, the fees are pretty low, many of them are about 1 dollar a month. Many people will tell you that these fees are too high. The reason is that they are looking at the amount of money that you are investing each month. For example, if you invest 5 dollars in your first month you are paying a 20% fee. Of course, the more that you invest the lower your fee percentage is going to be, but the fact remains that it is a dollar which is a great deal when compared to the benefits.

When a person starts using these investment apps, they will usually want to start learning more about the market. For me this was definitely the case.

Millennials are very hesitant when it comes to investing, however, when they start investing with these platforms and start learning more about the market, they find that investing can benefit them.

Of course, there are downsides to everything that we do, and micro-investing does have a downside. Because you are investing such small amounts of money chances are you are not going to get rich. Micro-investing is a great way to get started but if you are wanting to see a hefty return you will need to invest more. Of course, you can invest as much as you want on the platforms.

If you do decide that you want to invest more, you need to be aware of any fees that you will have to pay. When you are only investing small amounts, you will find that you pay small amounts in fees but when you increase your investment you will have to pay more. You do not want the fees to eat up all of your returns.

Micro-investing ensures that anyone can start investing. There was a time when you had to have no less than 500 dollars if you wanted to start investing. Today, using micro-investing platforms, you can start investing with just a couple of dollars. This means that investing is no longer only for the rich but for everyone that has some spare change.

There are plenty of platforms out there to choose from so let's take a look at the best ones.

1. Acorns-

This is the largest and the most popular of all of the micro-investing platforms. You can link your debit cards and your credit cards to the app which will allow Acorns to round up your purchases and invest the change. Each dollar will then be invested in one of the five ETF portfolios depending on what your risk tolerance is.

They also have a type of cash back rewards program that is called Found Money. This is a shopping portal that you can use when you are buying online. The retailers will then invest a percentage of what you have spent into your Acorns account.

Acorns does cost 1 dollar per month to use. Once your balance reaches 5,000 dollars you will have to pay .25 percent each year.

If you are a student with a .Edu email address you can use Acorns for free for four years.

2. Stash-

This is another micro-investing platform that is very popular. Stash makes it very easy for new investors to start investing in companies that match their beliefs. You are able to create your portfolio based on what you believe in such as clean energy, travel, and social media. This is a really great option for those that want to invest in a specific industry but do not have a large sum of money to purchase stocks.

You determine how much money you want to invest each month and all of the trades are free. In order to get started you are going to need to deposit 5 dollars. The fee is 1 dollar per month until your account reaches 5000 dollars and then you are charged a .25 percent fee.

3. Robinhood-

This is a completely free app that is used for trading stocks. There are no fees or commissions. If you want to have access to trading after hours or to trade options, you will have to pay a fee of 10 dollars a month. Most investors are not going to have to pay anything when they use Robinhood though.

While Robinhood is free, it does not offer any portfolio advice or investment research advice. And it is a mobile-only app.

This is the cheapest option if you want to purchase individual stock, however, you should still hang on to your broker.

Robinhood is different than Stash and Acorns because it doesn't buy or sell fractional shares. This means that if you want this option you are going to have to choose a different platform.

There are plenty of other apps out there that are good for different investment styles, but these are the top three investment apps.

Micro-investing is a great way for anyone to start investing. You have to remember that the best time for you to start investing is probably 10 years ago, or when you were still in school. The second-best time for you to start investing is right now.

The sooner that you start investing the more time your money has to make more money. When you are investing using micro-investing platforms there are a few things that you will want to do in order to boost your returns.

The first thing that you want to do is to automate. If the platform allows you to link your debit cards to use spare change to invest, do it. Make sure that you are investing more than your spare change though. Set up an automated investment each month. Acorn for example, will allow you to automate your investments each week or month starting with as little as 5 dollars.

When you combine the automatic deposits with the roundup you are going to see that you are investing more therefore increasing your chances of getting a good return. Of course, since you are paying a fee you also want to make sure that your investments are more than what the fee is so that the micro-investing platform is worth your while.

Boosting round ups is an option that you can also take advantage of. When you take advantage of the round up you will be investing your spare change whenever you use a card that is linked to your account. This means that if you spend 7.50 at lunch tomorrow, 50 cents is going to be deposited in your investing account.

Some platforms are allowing you to boost your round up by as much as 10 times. Meaning that instead of 50 cents being deposited into your investing account 5 dollars would be deposited. This is a great way for you to get into the habit of saving as much money as possible each day. However, you do not want to put yourself in a situation where this could hurt you.

When you are first starting out automating deposits and using round up is a great idea, but I would personally wait to boost the round ups.

Acorn also offers Found Money. You probably noticed that I am focusing on Acorn a lot here because this is the platform that I personally use which allows me to have some extra knowledge about how to increase your returns.

Now, back to Found Money. Found money is like the money that you find on the sidewalk when you are walking into the store. However, instead of finding it when you walk into the store you get it back for shopping through the platform online or by using your linked card at one of the retailers that works with Acorn. The retailer is going to invest a bit of money into your Acorn account just for shopping with them. These are businesses that you shop at every day, not random companies that you do not know.

These include Walmart, Nike, Macy's, Sephora, AT&T, Walgreens, Bed Bath & Beyond, and Hulu just to name a few.

As you can see, linking your debit card can pay off big time when it comes to padding your investing account. You can find a huge list of all of the retailers that participate on the Acorns app. You have to make sure that your card is linked, which will only take a few minutes. Then when you shop at any of the partner brands money will be put into your investing account. It does take between 30 and 60 days for you to see the reward but there really is no reason for an investor not to sign up for this. It really is free money.

When you use the micro-investing apps you are going to be able to monitor your investments every day if you would like, most people however, check the app every other day. For me, I check it once a week a couple of days after my automatic deposit.

Remember you don't have any control over how the market behaves from one day to the next. There are going to be days when the market does really good and days when the market does really badly. The best way for you to get the best return on your investment with micro-investing apps would be over a long period of time. Think about it in terms of years not just days.

Remember when we talked about how important it is for you to not allow your emotions to dictate how you invest? This is true when you are using micro-investing platforms as well. Don't let it cause you a lot of stress. Never invest more in these platforms than you can afford to lose and instead of watching the platform like a hawk spend your time focusing on your other financial habits.

Before you start investing in micro-investing platforms you really need to take a look at where you are in your life, your career, and how your finances are doing. If you are living paycheck to paycheck, carrying a lot of debt, do not have a retirement fund, or an emergency fund, you need to start there.

You see, investing is more than just putting your money into companies and hoping that you see a return. It is about getting your finances set up in a way that you can benefit from your returns. If you are investing 100 dollars a month but you are paying 12% interest rate on a car, you would benefit more if you put that 100 dollars toward paying off your car. The reason is because the average return on your investment is only going to be 9 percent. Financially speaking it would be smarter to pay off that car and stop paying that high interest rate.

Your investment career starts with your personal finances. If you are further in your investing career, if you have your savings account, your emergency fund, your 401(k) and your debt is paid off you may be in the position to start investing with micro-investing platforms.

While many people would choose to leave their money sitting in the bank instead of taking the risk of investing it, you have to remember that with inflation, the risk of leaving your money in the bank is pretty high. Investing is a much better use of your money than tucking it away is.

If you are much further into your career, as in you have started investing in the market on your own and have been doing so while seeing good returns for a while, micro-investing platforms are not going to benefit you any. On the other hand, if you are just starting out, micro-investing is a great way for you to start growing your investments right now and can help you to create a diversified portfolio.

Micro-investing is a great way for anyone to get started investing and building a portfolio without having to deal with all of the headache of doing it all on your own.

Chapter Twelve: Compounding Interests

Compound interest is a great way for you to create a pretty decent sized nest egg if you are willing to put in the time needed. The best investments are going to have returns that are compounded. This means that no matter what the market is doing or what problems the economy is facing you can count on compounded interest.

Understanding Compounded Interest

In order to understand compounded interest, we must first look at simple interest. Simple interest is what is paid to you based on the amount of money that you have put into your savings account. For example, if you have put 10,000 dollars into your saving account and your bank is paying you in annual interest rate of 2.5% you will get 250 dollars put into your account.

This is a basic savings account. In other words, it is a low risk as well as a low return investment. While it is possible for you to make a little bit of money on your investment while keeping it in a simple interest savings account, you can see higher returns with compounded interest.

You see, with simple interest, you are going to be paid interest on the 10,000 dollars that you invested into your savings account year after year. So whether it is year one or year 12 you will gain 250 dollars in interest.

Compound interest on the other hand means that you are paid interest for all of the money that is in your account, whether you invested the money or the money was made from interest.

For the first year, you would not see any difference, you would still get 250 dollars in interest but in the second year, you would draw interest on 10,250 dollars instead of the initial 10,000 dollars. Meaning you would get 256.25 added to your account. Each year the interest amount would continue to go up instead of staying the same as it does with simple interest.

If you are going to have a savings account, leaving your money in the bank for a long period of time, and you are going to be drawing interest it is much better of an investment for you to focus on compounding the interest because while it may not be much in the beginning, after a couple of years, that interest can really build into a nice nest egg.

Chapter Thirteen: The Takeaway

Investing is something that was once thought of as only for the rich. If you had not earned a million dollars, chances were that you were not investing. While investing large amounts of money can provide you with a larger return it can also cause you to lose much more.

Investing is now something that anyone can do. It does not matter if you come from the richest families or if you are the average Joe, going to work every day in order to pay your bills. Investing is something that you can do.

You have to determine if it is financially wise for you to do so depending on your personal finances. If your finances are not in order, chances are that this is not a good time for you to start investing. However, if you have taken care of your finances, meaning that you have your savings account, your 401(k) set up, an emergency fund, and you have paid off your debt, you may be ready to start investing.

It is also important for you to take your personality into account. Are you going to be able to handle it when the market dips? Are you going to be able to stick with investing long term?

Today we find that most people are overwhelmed when it comes to thinking about investing. Why? The internet has filled us with so much information and investment advice that it can all seem very overwhelming. While the internet has made it much easier for us to invest, it has also complicated things a bit. Too much information can be overwhelming while not having enough information can cause us to make bad decisions. It is a very delicate balance.

Financial advisors are also wary of people who are eager to invest in the market when they know very little about it. Studies are actually showing that many people are actually purchasing stock as speculators today instead of as investors. Of course, they may call it investing but the truth is that they do not know anything about the company that they have purchased stock in.

It is perfectly okay to get into investing as a hobby. When you start investing as a hobby you have to make sure that you follow the same rules as any investor would. Just like with any other hobby you have to make sure to take the time to learn about investing first.

Investing As A Hobby

Before you can start investing as a hobby you have to make sure that you can afford it. Investing is all about money and when you are investing it is very easy for a person to forget about the actual cost of their investments, especially if you are investing for personal amusement.

When you are investing for fun you have to make sure that you are not playing with more money than you are going to be okay with losing. We all know that almost all hobbies will cost money but no matter what the hobby is, we have to make sure that our spending does not spiral out of control. The same goes for investing. Know what your limits are and make sure that you are sticking to your budget. Don't take unnecessary risks just because investing is just a hobby for you.

Don't jump in too quickly. You have to remember, even if investing is just a hobby, that you are a beginner investor. When you are on the outside looking in, investing can seem very simple. But once it is your money on the line, things can get a lot more complicated. You have to understand that investing can be complicated and there is no secret formula that you can follow to ensure that you are going to see hefty returns.

Be aware of that. Especially if you are going to be doing research online. So many people get sucked into scams that claim to be able to provide them with the secrets to the market. These scams are going to do nothing except take your money and leave you wondering exactly what that secret was.

Making small investments can be a lot of fun and you don't have to worry about risking your entire savings or causing financial damage to you and your family. Speaking of financial plans, what are yours? If you don't have any financial plans that are long-term yet, you might want to think about that before you start investing as a hobby.

You wouldn't try to skydive without learning how to do it first would you? You would make sure that you knew everything about skydiving possible before you jumped out of that plane. Chances are that you would spend all of your spare time learning what the risks are and how you can avoid getting hurt.

The same should be true when you decide that you are going to invest as a hobby. You need to make sure that you learn as much as you can about it. While I have worked very hard to make sure that you have the best information possible in this book, and while it is a great place for you to start if you are interested in investing, there is so much more information out there.

If you have really paid attention to what is in this book, and your finances are in order, you are probably ready to start investing in small amounts. However, you have to understand that investing is something that you have to continually learn about. As long as you are investing you should be learning about investing. The more that you know the more successful you can be at investing.

Make sure that you understand what your risks are. You have to be very careful when you are testing out trading services. If a trading service is offering you a dummy account to do pretend trades on, they are trying to get you to believe that the risks and the losses that you are going to face do not matter.

While it is very important for you to practice or do mock investments, it is also important for you to make sure that you are tracking them and taking the time to learn from your mistakes. Every single investment that you make is going to have some sort of risk.

Investing as little as 100 dollars today could mean that I wake up tomorrow with 100 dollars less than I had today. The risk is real. The money is real, and it is very important for you to remember that.

When you first start out investing, even as a hobby, you want to focus on low risk investments. As you learn and become more comfortable with investing you can start investing in riskier assets.

Find the right place to get your investment advice. Today, it seems as if everyone has some sort of investment advice. People want to tell you their tricks and their tips even if they have no money invested. You have to remember that while a person may want to tell you how you should run your portfolio it is not their money that they are talking about.

You have to ask yourself, "Is this person a professional or an expert?" If not, they have no reason to be giving you investing advice. If they were as good at investing as they think that they are, chances are that they would be investing themselves and would be making a lot of money doing so.

Make sure that you have a financial advisor. If you are just starting out and you are using one of the micro-investing apps that we talked about in the last chapter, chances are that you are not going to need a financial advisor. However, as your returns grow, and you begin investing more and more into the market you are going to want someone that you know is on your side.

Using The Information That You Have Learned To Create A Passive Income

Creating a passive income can seem like a hard thing to do, however, investing can help you not only to create a passive income but to build your wealth as well.

You can use dividends as well as the interest obtained from bonds to create your passive income. This is going to provide you with an income as you continue to invest in the market.

Building your wealth is going to take a little bit of time, however, investing in the market is the way to go. As you watch the market climb, you are going to watch your wealth grow. Following all of the information that you have learned in this book is going to ensure that you are able to have a passive income while also building wealth in both the short-term and the long-term.

Now it is time for you to start making some decisions. It is time for you to decide what steps you are going to take.

Conclusion

The next step is to get out there and start investing. You now have all of the information that you need in order to get started investing and creating wealth for yourself.

By now I hope that you understand how it is possible for anyone no matter what their financial situation to start investing. Not only will you be investing in the market, but you are going to be investing in your future, your family's future, and your country's future.

By investing you are going to be able to increase your wealth while creating a passive income. But you are also going to be cultivating a skill that is very important. Learning how to invest in the market is something that a lot of people wish they could do. They don't realize just how easy it is. By learning how to invest in the market you are putting yourself 10 steps ahead of those who have not taken the time to do so.

Now it is time for you to start researching the companies that you are thinking about investing in. What companies do you want to put your money into? Start looking at their financial statements and follow the plan that you learned in this book to determine if the companies are a good investment or not.

If you still are not comfortable investing in the market on your own, you may want to consider doing a little micro-investing before jumping into investing on a larger scale. Getting your feet wet with micro-investing is a great way for anyone to start investing while minimizing their risks and learning about the market at the same time.

Micro-investing is a great tool for beginners to use when they first decide that they are ready to start investing.

Most importantly, just get started. Remember there is no reason for you to continue to put investing off one more day when you have all of these amazing tools at the tips of your fingers. Create your plan and get started. You are the only thing holding you and your finances back.

I want to thank you for reading Investing Basics: Learn the Stock Market, Build Passive Income, Grow Your Wealth. I hope that you have enjoyed reading this book as much as I enjoyed writing it for you and I hope that you have learned a lot as you have worked your way through the book.

Remember when it comes to investing, there is no time that you should stop learning. The more that you know about investing, the more your money will grow!

www.ingramcontent.com/pod-product-compliance
Lightning Source LLC
Chambersburg PA
CBHW020559220526
45463CB00006B/2374